ANIMALS THAT HAVE TOUCHED MY LIFE
Jeanne Sheeder Steele

Copyright © 2019 Jeanne Sheeder Steele. All rights reserved. No part of this publication may be reproduced or transmitted in any form or by any means, mechanical, digitally, electronically including photocopy, recording or any information storing or retrieval system without permission in writing from the author.

ISBN 9781093628586

Cover design and illustrations by Cindy Inman, Manns Choice PA
Editing by Loretta Radeschi, Bedford, PA

Prologue

I've been wanting to write this book for a long time, but just couldn't seem to get started. In the first place, I'm not a writer. This book will be written in my own words just the way I lived it.

I was born in south central Pennsylvania and lived on a small farm with Mom, Dad, Grandpa and Grandma. We had the usual animals - pigs, cows, chickens, and horses.

When I was three months old, my Grandpa put me on his old horse, Deck, and took me for a ride. From then on I loved horses and all animals, tame and wild.

Chapter 1

I was able to ride horses myself when I was five or six years-old. I would ride bareback. Deck was too old to go very fast. When he didn't want me to ride, he would pick me  up by the suspenders on my overalls. I just hung there with my feet off the ground until someone came and got me.

One of the things Deck did was unlock the lower half of his stall door, go across the dirt road to get a drink out of the water tub, then go back into his stall and relock the door. His stall was cool in the hot weather.

My Grandpa and I rode Deck after the cattle in the woods. Sometimes, they didn't want to come home, so my Grandpa went after them on foot. He told me to just stay on Deck's back and that I would be fine. Deck took me back home and stopped at the barn door. I put him inside and would go to the house. Deck was a good horse. He died at age 36 years-old.

Chapter 2

After we lost Deck, we had to get another horse to plow the fields. I was about 12 years-old. I say that because I remember working in the fields. I pulled weeds all day. When I got to the end of one row, there was another long row back. My  friends were in the swimming hole calling for me to come and swim, but I had my chores to do first.

It was some time before we found another horse. A nearby farmer had a sorrel horse. He bought a bay horse from another farmer to make a team to work the fields. Some time after he bought the bay horse, the farmer decided to sell him. That's how we got our second horse. Grandpa rode him home a few miles through the woods. I was allowed to name him and I called him Tony. He was about 1500 pounds with a white star.

Tony was five years-old and very smart. He and I became best friends. I taught him a lot of tricks. He would stand on his hind feet and would dig the ground with his front hoof to tell us how old he was. He'd take my grandpa's hat when I asked him to. When Tony wasn't working in the fields, we would go riding in the woods around our farm. He would jump the logs and streams. I had a little terrier dog named Teddy. He went with us in the woods. I would get off and lay on the soft moss and eat tea berries. Teddy would hold Tony's reins while Tony ate grass. In the winter, Tony and I would play in the snow. He would never hurt me intentionally.

I put Tony in a pasture on the side away from our yard. I would stand by him with my hands on my knees and say "Are you ready?" Then I would run up the hill and he would run, too. I would stop and so would he. Sometimes his hind legs would slide and almost throw him down. Then we would both run the other way. We would do that for a while. When we were done, I would pet and love him. We had a lot of fun. I taught Tony to walk sideways and cross his front legs.

My grandfather said he couldn't get Tony to work in the field like a horse should. I would talk to Tony and he did what I said, like pulling hay in the hay mower with a hay fork. When Tony pulled the fork, it would pull him side ways so my grandfather told me to tell him when to pull so no one would get hurt. That worked out fine.

When Tony and I worked in the fields, we both got hot so when we were done that we headed for the swimming hole right below our farm. Tony went in, too. My friends and I would get on his back and jump or dive into the water. When we were done, I changed my clothes and it was time to feed Tony. Then I turned him out to pasture to graze and rest.

In the wintertime I would take Tony out to get a drink every few hours. I had to put a halter on him attached with a long rope because as soon as he was out of the barn door he was up on his hind feet pawing the air. Soon he would settle down and I would take him to the creek for a drink. He was happy to be out of the barn and wanted to run a little so we ran before I put him back in the stable.

Chapter 3

We had chickens too. We had one large white hen that was blind. She became friends with a small black hen. They were buddy-buddy. When the black hen found something special on the ground,  she called the white hen to share it with her. The black hen was the white one's eyes. They went everywhere together.

We had a grape vine that was about 40 or 50-feet long. Where the vine was rooted in the ground, it went straight up for about four feet then it went straight out for about four feet. The black hen was often sitting on the vine while the white hen was on the ground. The black hen talked to the white hen and she flew up on the vine and sat with her. I just happened to be watching them. They did that often.

The white hen would follow the black hen to the hen house and jump up on the roost with her. She also found the nest to lay her eggs. They both drank together and ate together. It was something to see. It just shows you animals and birds are wonderful and how smart they are.

Chapter 4

As a young girl, I had to help milk the four cows we had. It wasn't one of my favorite jobs. I did like it, though, when our barn cats lined up in a row behind the cow I was milking. I would squirt milk at their faces and they would lap it up. Then they would have a good time washing themselves.

I always liked it when the calves were born and I would help wean them by putting my fingers in some milk in a bucket. The calves would suck my fingers and before long they were able to drink out of a bucket by themselves. Working in the barn wasn't all fun because I had to muck out the stalls and feed the animals.

Chapter 5

We had barn cats and a very small dog, white with brown spots. Her name was Mickey. She was our house dog. 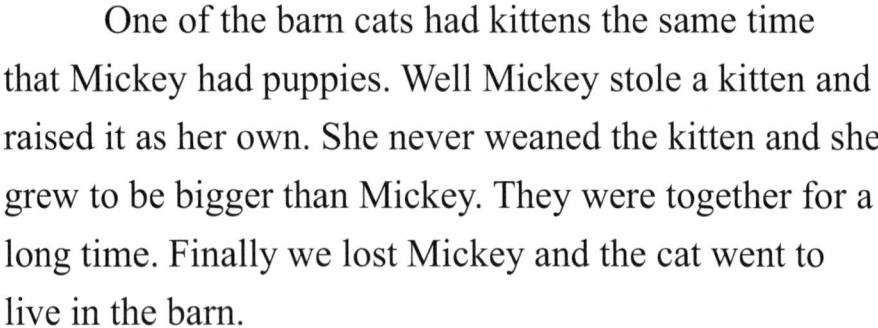 Mickey had some puppies, but I don't know what happened to them. I think my grandfather knew.

One of the barn cats had kittens the same time that Mickey had puppies. Well Mickey stole a kitten and raised it as her own. She never weaned the kitten and she grew to be bigger than Mickey. They were together for a long time. Finally we lost Mickey and the cat went to live in the barn.

Mickey had an earlier litter and we kept one of the puppies. He was white with bright brown spots and we called him Trixie. He grew up with us kids as I had a brother and sister later on. Trixie was always with us kids. Trixie would pinch my brother's legs until he'd let my sister and I go. We all loved Trixie.

Chapter 6

While I lived on the farm and had Tony, we lived near a mining town. Most of the people living in town worked in the coal mines. There was a large barn near the coal  mines that housed a lot of mules that were worked in the mines. There was a large yard built with a board fence around it for the mules to stand in. They had a large water tub to get a drink.

Every once in a while the mules would break out of the fenced area and head for the woods. The miners would have an awful time trying to round them up and get them back to the barn. They had one mule they called Kicking Jack. He was a small red mule with a temper. The miners had quite a time harnessing him to get ready to go to work in the mine.

When the mules broke out, the miners came to get me and Tony to hunt them. A lot of people don't know that a mule will follow a horse. They love horses. Tony and I would head for the hills and when we found the mules, we just headed for the barn and the mules followed us. We walked in the gate and the mules would follow. The miners would shut the gate and the mules would be safe at home. I always like going after the mules because Tony and I got to go for a ride in the woods.

Chapter 7

We had pigs on the farm too. One pig we kept in the barn across from the cows. When Mom fed the barn cats table scraps, the pig would stand up on his hind feet and Mom would feed him with the spoon. He  loved that. You know what happens to pigs on a farm, so we didn't want to get too close.

Neighbors that lived down the road from us had pigs and one of the sows had babies. Somehow one of the babies got its neck cut. The people brought the little one to me to see if I could do anything for it. I washed its neck with warm soapy water, rinsed it out with peroxide, dried it and put on an antiseptic powder.

While I was taking care of it, I would sit on the ground with a baby's bottle and say "Come to your mother," and it would run and jump on my lap. I often thought that if the baby grew up to maybe 300 pounds I would have had a lapful. At night I wrapped the baby in one of my old sweaters and laid it in a box in the shop right off our back porch.

But the pig couldn't recover and I lost the baby. In those days we didn't have vets like we do today. I cried about the loss.

Chapter 8

When my grandparents got old, my Grandma died and my Grandad sold our farm and we moved to a small town about three miles away. That meant my Grandad had to sell Tony. A farmer about 30 miles away bought him.

After Tony was gone for a while, Mom and Dad took me to see him. I had to walk down a lane to get to the field where he was. Tony was with another horse. I called him and he came on a run. The other horse came too, but Tony wouldn't let him get close to me. I was so happy to see him, but not the shape he was in. Tony had two big sores on his shoulders. One on each side.

When I had Tony, his mane, tail and face top were long. His face top was down to the end of his nose that kept the flies out of his eyes. I kept Tony washed and clean and the long hair was black and shiny.

I went back to see him a few more times then the farmer sold him. I didn't know where he went and I never got to see him again. It made me sad. I bet he wondered what happened to me. He's gone now. I loved him so much and I think of him often.

Chapter 9

Mom, Dad, my brother and sister and Grandad moved to town with our two dogs, Teddy and Trixie, so I had two dogs to play with. By that time I was in grade school. I had taught Teddy so many tricks like sit, beg, speak, roll over, jump through my arms, bring back a ball or stick, give me a kiss, dance on his hind feet around a ring and more.

A carnival came to our town and set up in the ball field. Some of us would go over there to watch them get the carnival ready. I took Teddy with me. We talked to some of the people and they wanted to see Teddy do some of the tricks that I told them about. So I showed them.

When the carnival left town, we couldn't find Teddy. My Dad and Grandad went to the next town where the carnival was.

There was Teddy . The carnival boss had taken him. When my Grandad called Teddy, he wanted to stay with the other man. This man loved Teddy, too, and treated him like royalty. This man told my Grandad Teddy would stay with him at the best hotels and travel with him in his own car, so my Granddad let Teddy stay.

We still had Trixie. She and Teddy didn't get along. They were always fighting so maybe Teddy was happier with the other man. Too bad because I missed Teddy. He was my buddy too.

Chapter 10

We had some cats while we lived in town. One was a calico and she was Mom's cat. She would jump from the back porch  roof to the shed roof when Mom asked her to. She was always in Mom's lap when she sat on the front porch.

I got twin boy kittens. They were gold colored and looked exactly alike. They were angoras. When they grew up, one cat filled the seat of a chair. They were very close like twins are. The cats went into the woods behind our house one day. One cat came home; the other one didn't until two days later. Some one had shot him in the shoulder. I took him to the vet and his wound finally healed.

When I brought him home, the cats were so glad to see one another. I had an idea who was shooting the cats around town and I was right. A year or so later the young man died in a car accident. The cat killing ended. My cats lived to be very old.

Chapter 11

When I was 14, work was getting scarce around where we lived so we moved to Black River, Maryland near Baltimore. Dad got a  job working on roads called the clover leaf. We lived in a summer house along the side of the bay. We could go swimming and sailing. My sister, brother and I had a lot of fun that summer and into the fall. The neighbors next door had a dog and she had puppies. Mom got us one. He was black with white on his face, chest and feet. We called him Scrumptious. From the time we got him, Mom would sit him on his hind legs on a kitchen chair before she fed him. While Mom was getting his food ready, she would look at Scrump and he'd be sitting up by himself. It didn't take him long to learn that trick. As he grew older, he made a good dog to play with. Dad's job ended so we moved back to Pennsylvania. We found a place in the upper part of a two-story house. The people that lived downstairs had a lot of kids so we all played with Scrump.

Chapter 12

The time came when we had to move to Warren, Ohio. Dad got a job working in the steel mill there. He and Mom found a place to live in a housing project. Of course we 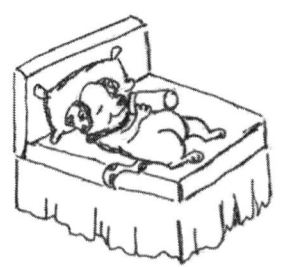 had to leave Scrump behind. The people downstairs kept him so he felt right at home. They kept him until he died.

We still had Trixie when we moved to Maryland and then to Ohio. We lived there about three years. It was right after World War II had started. Dad was past the age to be called to fight. That's why he wanted to work in a steel mill, to help the war effort.

I found some people that had horses so I could go for a ride once in a while. We made some friends while we were there. I can tell you I hated their schools. But I had to go.

One day my brother a playing with some other

boys on a dump where they burned things. They heard puppies crying and found three puppies in a cardboard box next to the fire. They were only a day or so old. The boys brought them home and we picked one to keep and some of the neighbors took the other two.

The one we picked was a little terrier white with brown spots on her ears and by her tail. The other two were white with brown spots. Our puppy was a female and we called her Wimpy. Mom went to town to get a doll baby bottle and nipple. It worked fine. We had to feed Wimpy every few hours. Mom made her a little bed to sleep in.

After she got a little older, Wimpy would come for her bottle, take it to her bed and feed herself. She grew to be a beautiful little dog. Since we raised her from a puppy, she knew everything we said to her. Trixie was still with us.

Chapter 13

Finally it came time to move back to Pennsylvania. We moved back to our home in our little town. We lived there for a few years. Trixie died while we were there. Wimpy was getting older and smarter. If we were going to carry water and didn't want her to know, we had to spell it. Anything else we wanted to do we would spell it. It got so she knew what we were spelling. One lady that stopped at our house said it wouldn't surprise her if Wimpy talked.

We moved again. Dad got a job in the steel mill at Levittown, Ohio. Wimpy was getting pretty old by then. Mom would wash her blankets and put them on the line to dry. Wimpy would sit under her blankets until they dried and were put back on her bed. One day three large dogs were heading into our yard. Mom saw this and thought they would kill Wimpy.

To Mom's surprise, Wimpy went toward them growling and with her teeth showing. And believe it or not, they ran. Mom said Wimpy was either awfully dumb or awfully smart. Mom was so glad. She grabbed Wimpy and took her into the house.

    Wimpy got hard of hearing, and when she went out we would clap our hands. She could hear that and would come. One night we left her out before we went to bed and we couldn't find her. We clapped and called but she didn't come.

    The next day I was driving up and down the streets to try to find her. On one of the streets closer to town, I found her lying along the road. She had been hit by a car. We knew she never went there by herself. Across the street from there lived some boy old enough to drive and we thought he drove her there but we couldn't prove it. Wimpy had a terrible beginning and a terrible ending. She loved the woods so we found a nice spot and buried her there.

Chapter 14

My brother got a job in the steel mill too. One day he asked me if I wanted to go horseback riding. He took me and a couple of his friends to a riding stable. They gave me a horse called Little Red.

These horses learned a lot of bad habits. I got on and off Little Red to check my stirrups and she swelled her sides out to keep the saddle on. After we started to ride, her sides went down to normal, but the saddle was loose.

We got on an old road where the grass grew along two sides. We started to run and my brother's horse's head was at my horse's rump. There was a large bush growing by the side of the road. Part of the bush was leaning out into my path. I leaned away to miss it and the saddle turned with my foot stuck in the stirrup. I was dragged 150 feet with my head dragging on the ground.

My hair was long and got mixed with dirt. The grass made a cushion so my head didn't get cut. But one eye was knocked out onto my cheek. My ear drum was broken and two vertebrae in my back were broken. My boot came off and I lay on the road. My brother got his car and took me to the hospital.

I was unconscious for four days. When I came to, I remember the doctor's nose against my nose looking behind my eyes, so they said. The doctor said my brain looked like a large blood clot from being bounced around. I was in the hospital for two weeks.

When I came home, I found I had lost my balance. It was hard for me to walk. Eventually as I was getting better, I learned to walk straight.

Chapter 15

I had been dating a fellow for about three years. He came to see us in Levittown, got a job and stayed for a few months. Then we moved back to Pennsylvania and got married. We lived in the house  Mom and Dad owned. They stayed in Levittown because Dad was still working at the steel mill.

Sparky (my husband's nickname) and I got a collie mix dog. When we were bringing her home, she rode in the back seat of the car. I looked at her and she looked so sad. We called her Happy. She was such a nice dog. She never did anything in the house.

Sparky and I were poor and we couldn't afford a TV. Sparky worked 3 p.m. to 11 p.m. in a coal mine. As I waiting at home, I braided rugs and sewed them together. Happy laid on my feet. While Sparky was at work, I trained Happy to bring his slippers when he got home. Happy ate out of a pie pan and I taught her to get the pan and sit by the table with it in her mouth. When she closed her mouth, the pan would fly up in front of her face. When she opened her mouth it would be straight in front of her nose. It was funny watching her and we would sit and laugh at her.

Chapter 16

I went in the hospital having our first baby. It was a girl. I told Sparky to go home and take Happy out to relieve herself, and not to let her out by herself. But,  course, he didn't listen and Happy got pregnant. She had ten puppies, five pairs that looked exactly alike. I didn't have a hard time finding them homes. They were very pretty.

After a while Sparky, our daughter, Sherri, and I had to move to Levittown to find work. We moved in with Mom and Dad. Sparky was a very good mechanic and found a job taking care of large trucks.

After we had been there a while, some people back home decided to sell a garage we had been trying to buy. So we moved back home again. When we moved to Levittown, we left Happy with Sparkey's mom and dad. Someone saw her and wanted her so they gave her away. We never saw her again.

Chapter 17

We got a small horse for our daughter when she was about four years old. We tied the horse out to eat grass and every time I looked at her, the rope was wrapped around her  legs. I would say "Are you having troubles?" We named her Troubles. She was brown and white, and had never been ridden.

I broke her because I didn't like the way a young fellow was doing it. She was easy to break so I just took it easy. She was afraid of the squeak of her saddle. I put the saddle in the feed entry and I would scrunch it until she wouldn't move and wasn't afraid of it. I would ride her because I was young and thin then. I would sing to her when we went riding. Troubles would put one ear back while I sang. When I stopped, she would turn her ear ahead. It made me laugh.

Troubles would open her gate from her pen in back of our service station and come into our store for her ice cream cone on a stick. I'd hold it out to her. She could take the ice cream off the stick as slick as a whistle. Then Troubles would go back to her paddock. She opened the gate by pushing it, and the spring would stretch.

We later kept Troubles in a small building at our brother-in-law's house. He lived a short distance up the the road from us.

We had to cross a bridge about 20 feet long. One evening we had Troubles tied out to eat grass. Sparky was going to take her to get her supper. They had to cross the bridge. I told Sparky to take a hold of her long rope up close to her halter. She had about a 15-foot rope. Sparky didn't listen. Instead, he took hold of the end of the rope. Troubles was going to eat and I knew she would hurry. They started walking and Troubles began to run. I swear when Sparky hit the bridge he had one fast step in the middle of the bridge. He was going too fast. The next time he listened to me. He didn't know much about horses.

We had built a barn for Troubles. She never did her business in the stable. We had an old toilet in one corner of her lot and she would run over there when she had to go. She went behind the toilet.

While Sparky was trying to paint her barn roof, he would stick the paint brush with the handle in his back pocket. When he came down to move the ladder, Troubles would sneak up behind him and steal the brush from his pocket and run with it. Sparky would chase her. She wouldn't stop until Sparky got close to her, then she would run again. Sparky would call to me to tell her to give it back. I would let her play for awhile then I would tell Troubles to give it back and she would. We were buddies and I loved her.

We had Troubles for a few years and Sparky sold her because he said she was mean with our daughter and he was afraid Troubles would hurt her. Believe it or not, Sparky sold her to the same person who bought Tony. He bought her for his son. I went to visit her several times. They never had her feet trimmed and they looked like skis. They sold her later on and I don't know where she went. I never saw her again.

Chapter 18

We got a big dog that had a lot of long hair. The hair was very thick. He was light brown with a black muzzle. We named him Rebel. He stayed in Troubles' barn. We made a hay bed for him. He was very comfortable. Our home was about a half mile from the barn and our garage. Sparky would go down every day to work.

One morning Sparky went down to work and Rebel had gotten hit by a car. His back leg was hurt. He couldn't walk on it. We took him to the vet. We brought him home to rest and gave him the medicine the vet gave us. After a few weeks, Rebel got an infection in his hip. One morning Sparky went to work and Rebel was gone. We hunted everywhere for him, but couldn't find him.

About a week later a small boy stopped in the garage and told us a dog was lying in the creek at the end of our property. We went to look and it was Rebel. He was so thin because he had't had anything to eat for several days. We gathered him up and took him to his bed in the barn. We gave him some food. He was so hungry. All the infection was gone.

Rebel was s smart dog. The creek had sulphur in it and that drew the infection out. The sulphur in the creek came from the mining town we lived in.

Rebel got better, but never would walk very well on his back leg. His shoulder and front legs got larger. He didn't seem to be in any pain so we were happy about that. We kept Rebel until he passed away. He was a happy dog.

Chapter 19

After Rebel died, our daughter wanted another dog so we went looking for one. We heard of a collie dog that had puppies. We went and picked one out and brought him home. He was so thin because the biggest puppy in the litter ate most of the food. I felt sorry for those puppies because the owners didn't make the large puppy stay back so the thin puppies could eat. I don't know what happened to them. I hope the owners gave them all away to better homes.

We called our collie pup, Bimbo. Our daughter, Sherri, loved him and they grew up together. As they were growing up, they played together. Sherri would play in the sand pile. Of course Bimbo was there with her. Sherri would pile sand on his head and it would run down his nose, the side of his head and his eyes. He kept his eyes closed.

We lived along the main road with a sidewalk between the road and our lawn. If Sherri would play too close to the road, Bimbo would walk close to her and walk her back into the yard. When it snowed, we would hitch the sled to Bimbo and he would pull her on the sidewalk and side road with us along, of course.

One day Bimbo was in the back yard and Sherri was in the side yard playing. All of a sudden Sherri let out a scream that you would think someone was hurting her. Bimbo was there in a few seconds. He smelled her and looked her all over to see if she was all right. I was sitting on the porch watching this happen.

I was sitting on our front porch another day when a man came down the street and came onto my porch. He had been drinking and was talking loud. I told him not to come any farther and that he was talking too loud and was going to awaken Sherri who was taking a nap on the living room couch. He kept on coming and talking just as loud.

Bimbo was lying on the porch by the side of the

swing and in front of the kitchen door. Bimbo never made a noise. He gave a jump and hit the man on the side of his face and knocked him down. I called Sparky to come and take him to the doctor's office. I went along and Sherri was with us.

When we got to the doctor's, the man was still carrying on. The doctor told him if he didn't settle down he would give him something that would settle him. The doctor cleaned the wound, put medication on it and we took the man home. It was quite a day.

Sparky decided to move Bimbo's box from beside the maple tree to the lower end of our lot. The maple tree was just off our patio and porch. Bimbo didn't like it there. One night it stormed thunder, lightning and hard rain. I got out of bed to see where Bimbo was and he was running back and forth in front of his box as far as his chain would let him. I put on a jacket and went after him. I let him come into the house and sleep in the kitchen. I gave him a rug to lie on. He was so afraid of storms. He never made a sound or moved that night. He was so glad to be away from the storm.

There was a man by the name of Max who lived a block and a half down the street from us and on the opposite side of the street. Max liked Bimbo and would coax him to come to his house. I didn't like it but he did it anyway.

One night Max was going fishing for a few days and asked me if he could take Bimbo with him. I told him "No, he was my dog." He didn't like that very much. But he still coaxed Bimbo to come to his house.

One day Bimbo was crossing the road to get to Max's house and a car hit him. I was sitting on the porch when Bimbo came home. He wasn't acting right and I knew something was wrong but I didn't know what. I felt him all over and couldn't find any marks or blood. Just about that time Max came up the street and told me what had happened. Bimbo seemed to be sore when he walked but he eventually got better.

We had a cat that had kittens. The mother cat and the kittens were on the front porch and so was Bimbo, lying in front of our kitchen door. The kittens came over to Bimbo to see what he was. They came to his larger ruff he had beneath his neck, and when they smelled him they began to sniff and spit at him just like cats do. Bimbo never moved and pretty soon the kittens got used to him.

The first thing you knew the kittens were asleep on his ruff. When you talked to Bimbo, he would never move his head, just his eyes. He didn't want to waken the kitties. Don't you know dogs are very smart.

From the time Bimbo got hit by a car, he seemed to go downhill. One night I heard him whining so I got out of bed and went down to the porch. Bimbo was lying down and fluid was coming out of his mouth. I sat beside him and laid his head on my lap. He was dying. I stayed there til he was gone. He died the day Martin Luther King was shot, April 24, 1968. It was a terrible loss for all of us when he died. Bimbo was about 10 years old.

Chapter 20

It was a few years before we got another dog. I had become a professional dog groomer. One of the female poodles I groomed was going to have puppies. When they were born, I picked a puppy. She was apricot colored. I named her Anjou.

When I went to work, I took her with me because she had to be fed several times a day. When she was awake, I carried her in my apron pocket and when she was asleep I lay her on the couch in my shop.

By that time I had a four-year-old son, Brook. Anjou played with Brook as she grew older. When Brook lay on the floor in front of the TV, Anjou would lay on his legs. When his friends and he were playing in the yard, Anjou would play with them. If they had a ball, Anjou would catch it and run with it and wouldn't give it back.

When Brook was school age, he would lie on the floor doing his home work. If Anjou wanted attention, she would lie on his homework on her back so he would play with her.

If we went on picnics, Anjou would go with us. Everyone liked her. She was well behaved. I took Anjou to work with me every day. I kept my shop door open and Anjou would lie in front of the door and come over to me and touch me to let me know a customer was coming by. She loved to go to work with me.

My sister lived close by and we would stop to visit for a few minutes on the way home. Anjou liked that. My sister and her family had a little poodle named Gigi. She and Anjou would play. It was their everyday routine.

As Anjou got older, she developed diabetes. I had read that spayed female dogs would never get diabetes. So much for that. I took Anjou to the vet. She took some of Anjou's blood, had it tested and we learned that she had sugar. The vet had put her on insulin and told me how to give it to her. I had to test Anjou's urine every day with some strips that the vet gave me. Those strips would tell me how high her sugar was that day and I would know how much insulin to give her. Anjou would jump up on her favorite chair in the kitchen and lower her head to get her shot. I had to give it to her in the back of her neck. Afterwards, I would rub her neck and give her a treat.

Anjou lived to be 12 years-old. One night she got sick and in the morning I took her to the vet where she died. The vet said Anjou had a virus that dogs were getting. I don't know where she got it. Anjou only went outside to go the bathroom and came right back into the house. But we lost her and we all took it very hard. She was like one of the family as all our pets were.

Chapter 21

My husband was driving an old truck delivering oil from house to house. In one home an older lady had some cats that she kept in her cellar. She asked Sparky if he would take one home. She gave him a black Persian (my favorite breed of cats). She was nine months old and very scared. She walked on the top of the dashboard when Sparky brought her home.

I put her in the cellar for that's where she was used to staying. We called her Black One. When she and I were alone during the day, I would open the cellar door a little and leave it open. Of course I put cat food and water in the cellar. I would sit by the cellar door at times and talk to her. But she wouldn't show herself. I just kept sitting there and talking to her and calling her by her name. Pretty soon she sat on the steps where I could see her and she could see me. We did that for a while. Then I tore some paper, tied it on a piece of string and slid it down the steps.

At first she was afraid of it, but then she got used to it and began to play a little. Finally she would come closer to me. Then one day she let me pet her. As time went by she would come into the kitchen with me, but I had to leave the cellar door open a little so she could run down the stairs if someone came to the door or came into the house.

Slowly, Black One felt more secure with me and the rest of us. Black One would go the archway between the kitchen and the living room. I would tell her "No" and she would sit there and look in. She learned well for she never went into the living room.

One day she got outside through the cellar door. She stayed close to the house. As she got more used to our home, she would sleep on a cushioned chair on our front porch. If we had company and were sitting on the front porch and Black One wanted to go to sleep, she would sit in front of her favorite chair and look the person in the eyes who was sitting here. As soon as they left, she jumped on her chair.

In winter time, Sparky made a nice screened box beside the furnace for Black One to sleep in. He made a small opening inside the cellar door in the wall. We put blankets in the box. Of course she had kittens.

Some people who lived up on the hill above us had gotten a male Persian cat from a pet store in Baltimore. He was dark gray, long haired and they named him Shy. They paid $200 for him. He came down to see our Black One and he would stay with her until his owners came after him and took him back home. In a few days or a week he would be back. The two cats would walk side by side and their tails would cross. They made the prettiest kitties. They were all colors, even calico. I always found good homes for them. In fact, I had orders for kittens before they were born.

There was one time that I made Black One a cardboard box to have her babies in. I had company that day and we were having dinner when Black One came to the door and cried. I thought she wanted some food but she just kept crying so I let her in and she went right to her box and started to have her babies. Dumb me.

We had gotten another cat that was a male. He and Black One were friends and got along well. One day Black One had some kitties and I brought the box with them into the kitchen. Our male cat came in and looked into the box. You know male cats kill kittens, so I was concerned, but Black One didn't seems to care. He got in the box and laid down and cuddled the kittens and started to wash them. He was such a good cat. He came to us as a stray and stayed. Of course, we fed him and he got along with all the other animals.

Black One was with us a very long time. She lived to be 22 years-old. She had gotten thin but she still ate well. On her last day, I picked her up and held her. I put a blanket around her, and her two front paws were out of the blanket at the top. As I talked to her and loved her, she moved her paws to show me she was happy and knew I loved her. That night I put her in a box with a blanket and she died. All her organs had shut down. That's what the vet told us.

Chapter 22

One evening my brother and his family visited us. I turned the back porch light on and went out to feed the cats. When I came back in, my sister-in-law said to me, "Boy those cats make a lot of noise when they eat." I turned the porch light back on and there eating the cat's food sat the biggest opossum I had every seen. The cats were sitting there waiting for the opossum to get done so they could eat. I didn't know I was feeding an opossum. After that I had to put more feed out for all of them.

Chapter 23

One summer evening Sparky and I were sitting on our front porch when down the back alley and across the main road came a skunk, just taking a walk back to the creek behind our house.

We would see him almost every evening. He paid no attention to us, just went on about his business.

One evening instead of going up the back alley the way he had come, he turned and went along the main street in front of the house to the middle of town. I said to Sparky "I'll bet he clears Front Street." I don't know what happened to him for that was the last time we ever saw him. Too bad.

Chapter 24

When my brother was a boy, he raised rabbits. He had a white doe and a gold buck. They had babies that were gold with white on their face, neck, chest and feet. He had built rabbit pens in our back yard but something killed all the babies except one. So I brought that one into the house to keep it safe. I housebroke him and he acted just like a cat or dog. He would follow you around.

We had coal stoves back in those days and a wood shed and a coal pile back of our house. Buck (as I called him) always went with us to get coal and would come back in the house with us. One day Buck was in the back yard under a box my brother had built for him. It was made of light-weight board with spaces in between. We put him out there to eat leaves and when we went out to get him he was gone. Some one had stolen him. We never saw Buck again nor found out where he went.

Chapter 25

It was getting close to Easter when stores would sell colored peeps. Our daughter, Sherri, bought a pink one with her allowance. She brought it home and didn't know what to do with him. So I took him and put him in the sleeve of one of my old sweaters. He slept cuddled up there. I fed him bread and peep feed. Since he was pink we called him Pinky. But as he got a little older, his feathers became white so we changed his name to Binky. Of course I was the one that took care of him.

Chickens are very smart. While my kids were in school, l would lie down for a nap in the afternoon. I lay Binky on his side with his head on my arm and we would sleep for a little while. When Sherri would go upstairs to clean her room, she took Binky along and he would lie down in bed with his head on the pillow. We had a piano for Sherri who took lessons. She would call Binky to sit on the piano bench. She'd point to a key and he would peck it hard enough to make a sound. He played a one-finger song.

Binky liked to sit on my shoulder from the time he was a little peep. He could hide under my hair. I guess it was sort of like another hen's feathers. I would sit on the porch swing with Binky on my shoulder reading the newspaper. I would say to Binky "Look there, they are having a good sale on cars," and he would stretch his neck down to where I was pointing and make some chicken noises. The kids would come on the porch from walking down the street and ask me to make Binky read the newspaper.

When we went shopping on Saturday night, I would ask Binky to sit on the back of one of my kitchen chairs and he would. I put paper on the floor and he would stay there when we were away or all night.

After he got older, he spent most of the day in the back yard. While I worked in the kitchen, every few minutes Binky would come up on the back porch and look in the small hole we had made in the screen door. He was checking on me. I would say "I'm okay Binky," and he'd run back out in the yard. He liked to dust in the dirt under my maple tree. Chickens all like to dust in dirt.

We would take a ride on Sunday afternoons and Binky came along. He would sit between my legs facing me or sometimes on my shoulder so he could look out the window. One day we drove into a car lot to look at some cars. There were people out walking around checking out the vehicles. Binky was sitting between my legs where no one could see him and he would crow. Everyone looked around to see where the chicken was. I would scold Binky but he liked to crow, and he kept crowing.

At home, I would go out to the patio and sit on the lounge chair, eating a peanut butter sandwich. I called Binky to come get a bite. You should have seen him trying to swallow it. That was funny. Binky never ate chicken feed. When we had spaghetti, he would slurp it down with sauce running down both sides of his mouth. I would take some paper towels and clean his face.

I had a good friend who lived behind our house. We would visit each other from time to time. Sometimes I would go over and we would sit on her porch. Binky didn't like my going over there. He would walk from our porch to her porch and back to our house all the time I was there. When I would come home, Binky wanted me to sit on the swing so he could sit on my shoulder. We would sit there and swing. I would talk to him and stroke his head and back.

One day my friend, Emma, fell off her step stool on the porch. Binky ran back home. I didn't know that she fell until a few days later when Emma told me. Binky really didn't like her. To him, I spent too much time over at her house.

The people who lived on the other side of us didn't like Binky and some mornings Binky would roost on our neighbor's truck. It was warm outside so I let him stay out at night. We built him a pen with a place to roost but he didn't like to stay in the pen. We never closed its door so Binky could go outside. I was afraid that my neighbor might hurt him.

Colder weather was coming so we had to do something to keep him safe from my neighbor. We knew a farmer who had a lot of chickens. We took Binky to live on their farm.

I called them every day and learned on the third day that Binky hadn't eaten a bit of food. We went down that evening after Sparky came home from work. When we got there, the farmer had put Binky in the coop with his young hens. He had to put Binky under a bushel basket or the hens would have picked at him because he was strange to them, and he had started to eat chicken food. We went back home hoping everything would work out all right for Binky.

I called them every few days. They finally put Binky in the bottom part of their barn where they kept the other hens. He seemed to be happy there. He was the only rooster with all those hens. I gave him time to get used to living there before we went to see him.

On the way to the farm one day, I stopped at a corn field and got an ear of corn, shucked it and when we got to the farm, gave Binky some to eat.

At first he just looked at it, but since he hadn't eaten for a while, he tried it and ate all I gave him. I knew he would have chicken feed to eat at the farm.

I called him to come up to the window (they had bars on the window) to see me. I said "Binky, do you want me to scratch your ear?" and he held his head up to the bars for me to scratch.

He still knew me, so I asked him if he wanted to go for a ride in the car. He went to the door and came out. I opened the car door and he hopped in and sat on my lap as he always had before. We took him for a ride and when we came back, I took him to the barn door. Binky seemed happy to go in and be with all his hens. He was king.

I saw him a few more times and he finally passed away. He had such a good life but not like chickens had. I loved him since I raised him from a peep.

Chapter 26

I want to tell you about some spiders. When we would go on a picnic, there would always seem to be one that would come on the table where I sat. I knew what it wanted so I put a drop of whatever I was drinking close to it and it would go to the drop and get a drink. Then it would on its way. If you see a spider on your picnic, give it a drink.

I had a small inky dinky white spider that lived in my house for a while. He would come down from the ceiling and I would take my hand under him and tell him to get back up there before he got onto the floor and got stepped on.

One winter day I was mopping the kitchen floor. But first I have to tell you I had put my mop in the wash room so it wouldn't freeze as it would have if I had put it outside. I thought maybe the spider might have gotten in the mop. So I shook the mop hard but there was nothing in it. I put the mop in warm soapy water and rung it out.

I started to mop the floor and out rolled the spider. I thought I had killed it. I said to myself "They do CPR on people, why not on a spider?" So I put him on the window sill above my sink in the kitchen. I pushed lightly on its back but nothing happened. I turned it over and did the same on his tummy, and his legs started to move. In a few second he was up and going. Wonderful.

I had a close friend, Pearl, who wrote a column for our weekly newspaper and she put the story in her column. A few days later, people called me to congratulate me. I said "On what?" They said "Doing CPR on a spider."

So much for spiders.

Chapter 27

I finally got another dog. She was a seven-and-a-half-year old Chihuahua. I called her Cricket. She came to my door one morning and I let her in. She didn't look thin and was used to being in a house. I fed her and called some neighbors and found out who owned her. Her owner, named Judy, lived up the block from me. Judy came down and took Cricket home.

A few days later Judy called me and asked me if I wanted Cricket. I said yes. My husband said we didn't need a dog. I told him he knew I was an animal lover when he married me so I got Cricket.

Judy told me a man dropped the dog off at her place. The man that owned her beat her, locked her out in the snow and asked another man to come and shoot her. The man said he couldn't do it so he dropped her off at Judy's. When I found this out I was furious. I would like to know who the owner was and put him in a room with his hands tied behind him. With a ball bat I'd teach him how it felt being beaten. I never found out who the man was.

Cricket knew everything you said to her. When Sparky was lying on the living room floor, I said "Daddy's lying on the floor. Why don't you go in and jump on his back. It'll be nice and warm." She went right in and jumped on his back and lay down.

Cricket wanted to come in bed with us so I let her. Sparky said he didn't want a dog in our bed. I said "Okay." Well I left her down stairs in the kitchen and put a board over the door so she couldn't come upstairs. She cried and cried until Sparky went downstairs and got her and put her in bed with us. Cricket was happy. Sparky had to give in. He couldn't stand to hear her cry. He was soft-hearted, although he didn't want to admit it.

When the weather was cold, Cricket slept next to me. She was a warm ball of hair that warmed me up and kept me warm. Cricket was house-broken and was a perfect lady around the house. As I said before, we lived along a busy street and I trained Cricket not to go off the porch on the street side. I could walk up the street to get the mail and she wouldn't come off the porch to follow me. She would stand on the very edge of the porch and

stretch her neck out as far as she could so she could watch me, but never came off the porch.

    I showed her the boundaries of our yard and she never went any farther. You didn't have to go with her when she was let out because she knew where we was allowed to go. There was one spot out by the garage where she like to lay. It's a place where the sun would shine in our yard out from under the maple tree.

    When Cricket was about eight-years-old, she started wetting the bed so I got some pads for her. I took her to the vet. He took a blood test and told me she only had 20% of her kidneys working. I asked the vet if the kidney could have been bruised from the beatings she took. The vet said that was a possibility. Then I really wanted to tend to her first owner with a bat.

    I'm sorry to say the side effect of the kidney condition was that she didn't want to eat. I fed her anything I thought she would eat. She would eat a little bit. Then finally she wouldn't eat at all.

On her third day without eating, Cricket couldn't get comfortable in bed. On the fourth day she would barely walk. I called the vet to put her to sleep. I took her to the vet that evening, The vet wanted to know if I wanted him to take her back in his hospital room by herself. I told him I would go with her and hold her because Cricket would never leave me. I cried the whole time and cried all the way home. We made her a box with blankets and her sweater and buried her in her favorite spot in the yard, out by the garage in her sunny spot.

That was the first time I ever had to put an animal to sleep. I hope I never have to do that again. She was a wonderful dog, and didn't deserve what she had to suffer in her lifetime and the way she died. That man will pay for what he did to her.

Chapter 28

One summer we had real dry weather without hardly any rain. Besides feeding the birds seeds, the woodpecker suet and the humming birds sugar water, I had older bread to throw out for them. Our one robin couldn't find a worm so she pounced on the bread and ate it. She did this every day.

One day I was sitting on the porch and a robin was sitting in the corner of our lot next to the street. Just off the sidewalk was a hole in the road for the water to run off the streets. I happened to think that the robin had been there a good while and she's was trying to tell me something if I just had the brains to listen. I went out to where she was and she never moved. I went over and looked in that hole and saw her baby. There were bars over the hole close together. I couldn't get my hands down far enough to reach her baby. I went into the house and got what looked like a pancake turner but it was wider and turned up at the edge. I took it out and out and reached down in the hole and her baby hopped on it. I brought the baby up and gave it to its mother. It was so glad. The baby hadn't eaten for a while so the mother robin had to feed it. You have to listen when birds or animals try to tell you something.

Chapter 29

Another day I was sitting on my porch when two small birds, smaller than a wren, came and sat on the lowest tree limb next to the porch. They sat there and chirped until I finally paid attention to them. Their chirp was so soft it took a while to hear it. I said "What do you want?" and they flew to the next low branch. I followed them until they flew to my other maple tree at the lower part of my yard. There lying on the ground was one of their babies. I got my pick-up truck out of the garage, backed it up to the tree, got my ladder and put it on the back of my truck and put their baby back in the nest. If you listen and they trust you, animals and birds will talk to you.

One night I took my dog out to relieve himself and he ran over to the base of the tree and was wagging his tail. I went over to see what was going on and there sat a baby blue jay. He was soaking wet. His parents were teaching him to fly. I brought him in and dried him, then I put him on the couch beside my son. Brook broke some bread in small pieces and fed him. When we went to bed, Brook put the bird in a box for the night.

When we got up the next morning I told Brook he would have to take the bird outside. His parents would be looking for him. We went outside and his parents were sitting on the ground calling for him. I told Brook to open his hands and let him go. When Brook did this, the bird just sat on his hands and looked up at his face. The bird didn't seem to want to go. I told Brook to give him a little push. He flew on the ground. His parents went right to him and still tried to teach him to fly. Everything would be all right for them.

We had a lot of of wrens that came to our bird feeder. But as I already told you, I also fed them broken-up bread. If I sat down to eat supper and forgot to feed them their bread, they would fly onto the porch and sit in front of our sliding glass door. Our table was just inside those doors. I would have to stop eating and take their bread outside to feed them.

A little wren was sick and had the runs. It would come for bread on the porch because the other birds would fight with it at the feeder Every time I would see it on the porch, I would give it some bread .The bird got to trust me so when I opened the door, it would fly on my hand and eat the bread. Every time I would open the screen door, it came flying in on my hand and sat and ate. I didn't know what to do to help the wren, so I put Kaopectate on the bread and the bird would eat it. Then I would clean its rump and it would fly back out in the yard. I fed the bird for a good while. Then one day it didn't come back. I guess it died. It would have been an older bird by then.

Chapter 30

I had a little female chipmunk that made her home in my backyard. I bought unsalted peanuts to feed her. She would take them to her home and store them for winter. One day she came on the porch for nuts and I held out a peanut in my hand and talked softly to her. She was reluctant to come get it. But I just kept talking and coaxing and finally she took the nut and ran home.

Chippy, as I called her, was nervous about coming up to my hand. But after the first time she would come right up my pant leg, sit on my lap and stick one nut in each side of her mouth and one in the front and take them home. That was three nuts at a time. I looked in the encyclopedia to find out more about chipmunks. I found out their life span was only three years. I had Chippy for five years. She was protected in my yard.

Every spring I would look and see two little heads come up out of the hole where she lived. She would bring her babies on the porch and they would run around my feet and not be afraid. I kept a bowl of water on the cement blocks that made a wall around my patio for Chippy and her babies, and the birds to get a fresh drink.

One day I was in the house and I heard her chirping loudly and I went to see what was the matter. I thought there must be a cat around so I went clear around the other side of the house to check and didn't see one, but she just kept chirping. One thing Chippy had was a good hiding place between my plastic flower box and my cement flower box. I went back into the house but I kept watching Chippy.

I had a grill on my patio with a cover over it. I didn't know it then, but a white cat was hiding under that cover. The cat chased after Chippy and Chippy hid between the flower boxes where the cat couldn't get her. I chased the cat out of the yard and Chippy came back out. She looked me just as much to say "I tried to tell you." She was one smart Chippy.

A friend, John, was sitting on the porch talking to me when I saw Chippy. I told him to sit quietly and still so Chippy could look him over from a distance. Chippy looked at me and thought it must be okay, so she came up on my lap to get her peanuts and took them to her hole.

John said if someone had told him about Chippy, he wouldn't have believed them. He said he never saw a wild animal trust a human so much that they would get on the person's lap. As I said, I had Chippy for five years, but I never tamed another one.

Chapter 31

My dog, Cricket, had been gone for a good while and I missed her. Our church has a building attached to the back where we held our dinners on Thanksgiving, New Year's, Christmas and for reunions. Well, this day people from the church were having a reunion. My friend was married to one of them and attended the reunion. One of attendees had a female Chihuahua dog who had six puppies: two tan, three black and one brindle. They all lived but the runt who died. My friend told the lady with a picture of the puppies she was going to show it to me. I picked a pup and they gave her to me when she was seven weeks old. She weighed one and a quarter pounds.

I wanted to call her Tequila. My granddaughter said that's a drink with a worm in it and not to name her that. The ladies from church came to see her and they said, "Don't name her that." She was too precious.

My husband wanted to call her Missy Mouse. So her name became Precious Takela Missy Mouse Little Girl. I spelled Takela my way not the Mexican way.

She was real easy to house break. She slept with me every night and would wake me when she had to go out. I didn't want to feed her from the table, but my husband did and spoiled her. Now she wants bites when we eat. My husband, Bob, (I was married twice. My first husband died after 42 years of marriage), has a medium-size poodle and it's really his dog. I don't pay much attention to him. His name is Bubbles and he's well behaved and house broken.

Chapter 32

I heard on the radio that someone had a long haired Chihuahua to give away. I was the first caller and I got her. Her name is Amy. She's also a nice dog. She has long white hair with brown spots. When we watch TV, it's a good thing we have a long couch for Bubbles sits besides Bob. Amy is either on my lap or lying beside me and Little Girl is on me too.

The people that had Amy kept her in a room with food, water and puddle pads. They didn't pay much attention to her. But when their grandchildren came, they played with her so she loves kids. When my grandchildren come, they put her in a doll baby buggy and take her for a ride in our back alley. Sometimes they dress her up and put a blanket over her. She's usually sitting up like a baby. Her one bad habit is that she runs off if you don't have a leash on her. The people who had her before me let her run with another dog and didn't break her from it. You don't usually find little dogs that like children so that makes her special.

My little girl is three years old now. It doesn't seem like I've had her that long. Wherever I happen to be in the house, she's with me. I never go anywhere, including to the bathroom, by myself. When I'm in the tub, she stands up on the edge of the tub until I get out. She doesn't miss a thing. She's such a sweetie.

Chapter 33

I don't want to forget to tell you about my ferret. I went shopping one day and when I came home my son, Brook, and a friend were sitting on the kitchen floor holding a ferret. I asked him what he was thinking of. I didn't know how to take care of a ferret. I was running around the kitchen grumbling. It was going into the living room when I heard Brook say to his friend that I was upset now but tomorrow I'd be loving her. He knew his Mom pretty well. I had to take care of her. Brook named her Ashley.

We bought her a cage, a litter pan, a water bottle and a dish. She seemed to be cold so I bought her a hat like the kids wear in the winter time. She went down inside, turned around and slept with her head out.
I bought a book about ferrets and it said you had to have a litter pan in every room for them. Not Ashley, she would be in the living room with me and if she had to

go, she went through the kitchen to the wash room to her cage and litter pan. She was called a silver tip which means she was gray with all four feet white.

When I came home from work, I would let Ashley out of her cage and go into the living room to take a nap on the love seat. Ashley would touch my arm for me to lift her up. She would lie across my neck and sleep until I got up. Then she would be wherever I was - getting supper and whatever. When I was watching TV, she would lie on my shoulder. I would put her in her cage when I went to bed. Ashley played with me and never would bite.

When she had to go the vet, he said he didn't like ferrets because they were mostly mean. But he liked her because she was so nice. She was so lovable but the only bad thing is ferrets only live seven years so at the end of seven years I lost her.

Chapter 34

I've had several parakeets over the years. They all sat on my shoulder and would hide under my hair. One started to say "Pretty, pretty." Then I lost him.

All of them took showers on the divider between the double sink in my kitchen. I would let a small steam of lukewarm water spill onto the divider and they would shower. They got pretty wet. Then they would fly on my shoulder and dry and preen their feathers. The last one I had I would sit him on the coffee table.

My husband and all the dogs were on the couch. The cat on the rocking chair and we all took a nap. I would tell the parakeet to close his little sleepy eyes and he would. In a few minutes he put his head under his wing and was really sleeping. He got sick when he was only a few years old and died.

Chapter 35

I didn't have a cat in a good while and wanted a Persian. I heard on the radio on a program called The Trading Post that one was for sale. I met the owner halfway between our houses. She had him in a cage. She told me to bring a cage to put him in. When she lifted him from her cage by the back of the neck, she said he was wild and would claw me. After she left, I picked him up and cuddled him and he started to purr. He was not wild.

I took to the vet. He had sore ears, sore eyes and an upper respiratory infection and was about starved. I got him kitty food and milk. I didn't think he would ever stop eating.

Today he's fully grown and I call him Pussan. He's an apricot color and has a lot of long hair. He's an indoor cat and very loving. He goes into the bathroom with me. He also sits on the arm of the couch beside me.

I have a bow window in my living room and he likes to lay there. He sits in the window when the kids are going down the street to catch the bus. The kids stop and ask me what his name is. They see him every school morning. He's a very good cat. I only showed him the litter box one time and he has never messed in the house.

Chapter 36

It's been a long time since I had a horse. One day my son, Brook, went for a ride with a friend who had horses. When he came home, he told me he liked to ride and wanted a horse. I told him we would look for one. I would buy the horse and he could care of it. And as I thought, I ended up taking care of her most of the time because Brook had to work. He called her Sunshine and kept her in his friend's barn until we could get a barn built.

Brook built the barn by himself. Eventually he built three barns. This was his first. It had 10-foot by12-foot stalls and a place to keep feed. We kept the hay in the loft over the stalls. We could put about 100 bales up there.

Brook's girlfriend, Wendy, bought a black gelding and called him Midnight. She kept him in our barn. They would go riding.

I didn't have a horse to ride so I went looking for one. I found a Morgan mare and bought her. She was 15 hands and a chestnut color, with no white anywhere on her body. Her registered name is Lil Darling. I called her Lacey. She waa\s very loving and followed me when I'm in the horse pen. When I stopped, she'd put her head over my shoulder and I would kiss her on the nose. She didn't like to be led on a lead rope. If you didn't hold onto her halter, she'd run and pull the lead rope out of your hand. She wouldn't go anywhere but to the barn and wait until you opened the gate so she could go in. When I rode her, she listensed to everything I wanted her to do. I got a barn and a good horse when I got her.

Back to Sunshine. She was a sorrel with a white star and a snip on her nose. She was a small horse, just 14.2 hands. She was an Arabian and Quarter horse mix. One of the best horses I ever had. A child could ride her safely. When people came with small children to see the horses, Sunshine would put her nose out slowly, be very gentle and let the children pet her.

My son always rode Sunshine, and I always rode Lacey, but one day he wanted to swtich. While we were riding side by side, Brook looked over to Sunshine and said "You look small from up here and Sunshine turned her head away from Brook. She was insulted and she let him know it.

One day Sunshine stepped on a nail and got a really sore hoof. Brook soaked her hoof in a bucket of Espom salt and when the sore came to a head, our farrier cut it open and drained it. For a week or more we had to put penicillin on the hole where the nail had been until the hole healed and Sunshine could walk again.

She had allergies and I had to give her medicine for them. She coughed some, but she finally outgrew the allergies.

Sunshine had come up from Virginia on a cattle truck and was for sale. I went to see her and really liked her so I bought her. I don't know why anyone would get rid of such a good horse. My guess is she belonged to a young person and they sold her so they could buy a car.

You could lay the rein against either side of her neck and she would spin around until you took it away. You could ride her at a run, stop and let the reins fall to the ground and she would stand there. I think she was trained for the rodeo. She sure was a wonderful horse to ride.

The sad day came when she was 30 years old. Sunshine died from a heart attack. I thought I would have had her a lot longer than that. The vet said all those allergies and coughing were hard on her heart. It was hard to give her up. She was a big part of my family.

I had Lacey for several more years and would ride her. She would stand still when I slid off the saddle so I could get my arthritic legs straightened up. She knew my ways and I knew hers. We were a perfect pair.

Chapter 37

A lady that lives a few houses up from me in town had a two-year-old registered Paint for sale. She asked me if I would buy him. She said I was good to my horses and she wanted to get him a good home. The lady had three children and didn't have time to take care of him. I bought him.

He was laid back and easy to get along with. I was going to try to break him myself but I was getting older and if he would throw me and I got hurt, I wouldn't bounce back quickly as I would have when I was young. So I had him professionally trained. The trainer did a good job. He was supposed to be a Paint but he turned out to be a Bay with a star and white hind legs. His registered name is Tips Hotroddon Dude. I called him Dusty.

I sold him to a young man who had one horse and was looking for another. He had a good home on a farm with lots to eat and another horse for company.

Chapter 38

One day in May I bought a Rocky Mountain Gaited horse. The owner brought her up from Kentucky for me. He was also bringing another horse for a friend of his wife's.

The horse was 18 years old and very well gaited. She was seal black with a star, a small streak of white, a snip on her nose and two white hind feet. I didn't like riding a gaited horse as well as I thought I would. My friend loved to ride gaited horses so I let her ride her.

I called her Misty Blue. Her registered name was Three Sister Epoh Wendy. I didn't like that name so I changed it.

Chapter 39

A few years ago I bought a chestnut stallion from a family that brought him up from Texas. He was an American Midget horse, 31-inches tall. He was kept in the lower part of a garage with no windows. It was pretty dark. When I went to see him, they put him on a rope and he'd run and jump and lurch because he felt so good to be out. The owner wanted too much money for him and I told him what I would pay. He said "No" so I left.

A few weeks later he called me and said he would take what I offered, so I boght a midget horse. His name was Sweetie. After a few years, I went looking for a mare. I had a friend who raised and showed these types of horses. She had boxes and boxes of ribbons.

I called Ann and asked if she had any mares for sale. She said she only had one she hadn't bred and she was taking her to the sale. Ann told me she didn't know how well people would treat her, so Ann sold her to me.

Her name was Excited Lady. She had some flaws and was not show quality. She had a glaze in her left eye and a dip behind her withers (shoulders), so no one paid any attention to her.

When Lady was of age, she was with a stud horse and had a beautiful baby. Her owners back then had her registered so they could register her foals. Ann bought her and used her for a brood mare. Lady had beautiful babies for Ann and made her some money. She and Lady never liked the stallion she had her with.

But when Ann brought Lady to meet Sweetie, she just loved him. Lady laid her head on Sweetie and rubbed his neck to show her affection. They were together for a few years before she had another baby.

My husband, Bob, and I went down to the barn on a Saturday morning to feed the horses. I saw the baby standing beside Lady. I couldn't believe Lady had had a baby. The baby was not in good health. She couldn't stand up to nurse so I held her up to Lady. I was at the barn at 11 o'clock at night and returned every three hours, She was a beautiful foal, tannish gray in color.

I loved her, but she lived only three days. My vet said it was a bad year for all foals especially the midget horses. I still think about her. I named her Saturday's Surprise. I buried her in part of the horse yard under a tree. Well, enough about her.

Chapter 40

When my husband, Bob, and I lived in the same house I live in now, he saw ghosts living here with us. There were six of them. One was a tall slim, dark-haired man. There were two teenagers - a boy and a girl, and three small children.

Bob could see them and talked to them. He said they sat in our large living room chair and watched TV with us. The small ones sat in our large bean bag.

When my daughter took me to Port Matilda to stay with her for a while, I didn't like it there — no neighbors, no one to talk to on the phone. I got tired of living there and came back home.

When I got back home the ghosts were gone. And I never saw them again. My great-grandmother said this house was an old house when she was a little girl. I don't know who the ghosts might have been.

After Bob died, the ghosts still lived here with me. I couldn't see them, so they opened my top cupboard doors, and dropped my soap dish when I was in bed.

While I watched TV, my little dog climbed behind my neck and just shook. She knew they were there.

Chapter 41

It was wintertime and I went to the barn to feed my horses. As I was leaving, I shut the gate and looked down at the frozen grass.

There in a small block of ice was a four-leaf clover. I brought it home, thawed it out, dried it off and put it between two pieces of plastic and put it in my wallet.

I had it there for years, but finally it fell apart so I had to get rid of it.

I could never find a four-leaf clover in the summer time, and believe me I tried.

Chapter 42

I had a cat that I raised from a kitten. When he grew older and I was sitting on my porch swing in the summer, my cat would go hunting in the woods and catch a baby rabbit and bring it to me.

He would sit at my feet. I picked the rabbit up and would pet my cat and love him. When he went to lay down, I would take the baby rabbit back to the woods and let it go.

The next night or two, he would bring me more baby rabbits.

This happened all summer long. He was a loving cat and we loved each other.

Chapter 43

I can make a pet out of anything. One of them was a lady bug. This one flew into my house and I caught her and set her on my window sill above my kitchen sink. I fed her sugar water so she stayed there. I fed her when I ate.

After she was on the window sill for a while, she became real tame. She would be there in the day time. Then after supper I went in the living room to watch TV. I turned the light out in the kitchen and on in the living room. When I did this, the lady bug followed me into the living room and sat on the table that had my lamp on it. She sat there until I turned the lights out in the living room and turned them back on in the kitchen.

She followed me to the kitchen and sat on the window sill and I fed her some more sugar water and turned the lights out and went to bed.

When I'd get up the following morning, there she was sitting on the window sill waiting for breakfast so I fed her some more sugar water. This kept on every day until I found two very very small worms. I didn't know what they were and I found out later there were her babies. Finally they died and she died too.

I don't remember how long I had her. I don't know their life expectancy. I remember she was with me a good while.

Chapter 44

My last story is about a snake. I went down to the barn to feed the horse one morning. I had a 12-foot by 24-foot room. I had an area about four feet square upon which to set a metal can for sweet feed. In the rest of the area I put several hay bales so I wouldn't have to climb in the hay loft to get bales.

One morning I went to the barn to feed my horses. I opened a bale of hay and separated it to give each horse two or three slabs. When I went in, I saw this little snake. It came out from the back of the hay bales. It was about nine inches long and went in and out around my feet. It looked up at me like he would like to have talked to me. I spoke to it and said "Where did you come from?" As I was leaving, I saw the snake go behind the bales of hay.

Every time I went to feed the horses, the snake would come out and slither around my legs. If anyone else fed the horses, the snake wouldn't appear. It only came out when I was there alone.

The snake remained in the barn for a couple years, and always came out when I was there. It eventually grew to be about three feet long.

One morning I went to feed the horses and there was no snake. I couldn't imagine where it was.

My barn was about 100 yards off the main road. When I got to the road, there lay my snake. Someone had killed it. Why do people kill snakes that aren't poisonous? It would never have hurt anyone. I still think about that friendly creature.

Epilogue

I've lived in the country all my life. One day I stood at the end of a rainbow. All the beautiful colors fell on and around me. It was a great feeling. There was no pot of gold. It must have been on the other end of the rainbow.

I feel I'm a very blessed person.

I hope you enjoyed my stories and will always see the beauty and love in all of God's creatures.

So Long,

Jeanne Sheeder Steele

To purchase additional copies, please call 814 623-7399 or email lradeschi@centurylink.net.